The Day

The Day God Made

GLEN C. KNECHT

THE BANNER OF TRUTH TRUST

THE BANNER OF TRUTH TRUST
3 Murrayfield Road, Edinburgh EH12 6EL, UK
P.O. Box 621, Carlisle, PA 17013, USA

*

ISBN 0 85151 851 6

*

*

Typeset in 12 /14 pt Goudy Old Style by
Initial Typesetting Services, Dalkeith
Printed and bound in Great Britain
by Bell & Bain Ltd.,
Glasgow

DEDICATED TO MY WIFE, BETTY JANE,
WHOSE SPIRIT RESONATES WITH MY SPIRIT,
REJOICING IN THE LORD'S DAY.

Contents

Preface

1. Importance   1
2. Creation   9
3. Commandment   15
4. Christ   23
5. The Condition of Humanity   33
6. Holiness   39
7. Rest   45
8. Others   53
9. Permanence   59
10. Delight   67
11. Service   75
12. Instruction   81
13. Antinomianism   87
14. Consummation   95

Preface

IN THE LITTLE town of Oxford, Pennsylvania, where I served the Presbyterian Church for eight years, there is a 'village green', a little place in the middle of the village where only grass and trees may be found. No one may build there. It is reserved as an oasis of refreshment amidst the busy life all around.

It often made me think of the Lord's Day, as we have come to call the Christian Sabbath. For there, too, God has fenced off a little section of time reserved for the restoration and blessing of His people as they devote its hours to His worship and to rest.

Sadly 'the Day' has suffered the erosion of all kinds of forces arrayed against it. Some, when they think of it, call up images of legalistic and dreary days in a distant past. Seldom is it anticipated and loved and honoured by the people of God, the very ones who should appreciate it most.

Thus this little book, designed to be read on a Sunday afternoon, is offered with the prayer that the Lord of the Sabbath may choose to use it to promote the joyful use of this good gift of God.

I acknowledge my deep debt of gratitude to the editors of the Banner of Truth Trust for their kind and helpful guidance in the preparation of these pages, and to my beloved wife

Betty Jane for her patient and faithful encouragement in this and in all things good and spiritual. I am also indebted to many authors, read over many years, who increased my love and zeal for God's Day of Sabbath rest.

GLEN C. KNECHT
September 2003

I

Importance

I

Importance

A CRITICAL SITUATION exists in the world today. The spiritual
charter of men and nations has been abandoned, and we have
not realized it. We have slipped from the high pattern of
human life designed by our Maker and taught to us in the
Holy Scriptures. We have lost the Day separated from other
days by God.

This has had an impact on every aspect of life and the
environment in which we live. Families experience frag-
mentation, strain, and disintegration. The lack of opportunity
for life together in the home afforded by a right use of God's
holy Day means no organizing centre around which the
members of a family can mobilize themselves. The failure of
fathers and mothers to teach children the ways of God and
the wisdom of God from the Holy Scriptures and from life
may come partly from the abandonment of the Day of days.
Families are thus consigned to endless rounds of activity and
hurry with no hedged-about areas of time for leisurely conversation and the chances to impart the knowledge and love
of God to a new generation. Husbands and wives, robbed of
restorative hours on a regular basis on the Lord's appointed

Day, become irritable. Loss of temper in the home is a plague spoiling the effect of preaching and teaching in the church. Divorce has become accepted, when a quiet and worshipful Sunday spent together would perhaps have been a healing balm for wounded hearts.

Persons suffer as well as families. Mental and physical stress abound, so that hospitals for mental patients are full and new ones are needed. Traumas take great numbers of lives, many of these induced by stress and lack of moderation and proper respect for the rhythms of life. Loneliness is creeping into apartments and rooming houses where people lack the opportunity for leisurely conversation with families and with other like-minded friends due to the loss of a day for friendships.

The new disorder of our times is workaholism. But God's antidote has been disregarded. He calls us to stop one day in seven and to be identified other than by our labour. We are after all, far more than our work title would indicate. On that Day, as unique human beings made in God's image, our identity comes not by our doing, but by our being. That is the needed inoculation against the compulsion to evaluate ourselves by our work.

The loss of the Day leads to the loss of the church. First, the church weakens, then it compromises in order to attract, and finally becomes not the true physician of society but the charlatan of the modern age. Then it collaborates with the culture until it has no distinctive message to bring to a disordered time. When the Day is gone, the church is gone, too.

Yet all of this is from the point of view of human life. That is where we begin. But there is also the dimension of eternity and that is far more serious. For God made us, and He does not receive our thanks for that act of creation. The theory of evolution has taken the place of the truth of creation, and has received the attention that belonged to God's great creative act. We have forgotten how to be thankful, and God is grieved with us. He designed a Day for Himself in which we would have a block of time for rendering worship and thanksgiving and praise to Him. It was to be His Day in our lives, when the eternal dimension of our existence was most prominent and given due exercise. But we have counted this day much like any other and done our pleasure and fulfilled our needs and forgotten the One who gave this day as a gift of special quality to us. In the words of Patrick Fairbairn, 'The moral feelings and affections of our nature must have something outward and positive, determining the kind of landmarks which they are to observe, and the channels through which they are to flow.'[1]

The 'One Day' in seven might have been omitted and life been simply a cycle of sameness, but He placed in our midst a little oasis of greenness for meditation and rest, serving others and growing in understanding of His ways and His love. He made it for us, that the unique relationship which makes us different from other creatures might not wither or be lost, but that it might flourish and thus enhance and sharpen our humanity. It was truly His bestowing the Day on us which was the crown of all His creative acts. As if at the close of His activity, He added yet this, the setting apart of a day to honour and remember who is the Author and the Builder of it all, and to whom thanks and praise should be given.

[1] *Typology of Scripture*, vol. 2 (Grand Rapids: Kregel, 1989), p. 112.

The need remains and the will of God has not changed. What God bestowed on His first people, He bestows on us also; namely the establishment of the Day He set apart as His, and the right use of it in His service and for His glory.

The Day is a sign between Him and us – a sign that He has placed there as a special bond of holiness and love. The animal world knows nothing of it. The heathen know nothing of it without borrowing from His revelation to us. To profane the sign is to confess disrespect for the Signer. To disregard the Gift is to show disregard for the Giver. But our God is a holy God, who is known for His justice as well as His love. He will endure our disregard and our neglect for a long period, but He is bound to show His judgment in His own time. Some of that judgment we are feeling already, and we shall experience more and more unless we turn from our neglect of the Day which has been designated for Him and for us.

The judgment is inevitable because the violation of God's Day is a symptom of something deeper, which God will not tolerate. It is an indication of our inward pride, for we are professing that we know better than He knows and that we can order our lives better than He can. Our setting aside His will for the observance of the Lord's Day He sees as impure because what we actually do represents the syncretism of human reasoning and divine command. Such a joining of human values with God's standards is an adulteration of God's truth. God sees our practice as vanity, because it is empty of lasting results. Our machines wear out, our bodies break down, our families come apart, our resources exhaust themselves, and our God sees the vanity of the human perversion of the divine design. It is repugnant to God because it speaks to Him of our self-confidence and our ultimate trust in ourselves rather than in Him. We are not ultimately depending upon His pattern for human life, but upon our own pattern which we deem to be better for us. We do not rely on His wisdom, setting aside our own. Instead we rely on what we can do and thereby prove that we do not trust in His plans for us. That is reason for divine wrath.

What, then, is the concern of the hour? It is the recapturing of the foundations of the Day as they are laid for us in Holy Scripture. The foundations have been covered over by the dust of doubt, and obscured by critical handling. They must be rediscovered, for a true revival of anything depends not on emotion but on facts, and the foundations are factual and firm enough to bear the weight of a revival.

Such an undertaking must occupy us first, foundational as it is. But a structure rests upon it, and it is equally important. What is God's design for the Day? How did He envision the design when first given, and how does He see it today? The answers cannot come from fancy or conjecture, but need to be firmly rooted in Scripture study and interpretation.

Yet the hardest part of any biblical truth is the application we make to daily life. What is that to be? How shall it be implemented in secular societies that already consider the Christian somewhat out of step with the times? What will families make of the Day, in such a way as not to alienate but rather to cultivate the little ones that God has given them? How shall the church and the family work together in making the Day a real sign to the world that believers are distinctive? What is the key to observance that is pleasing to the Designer of the Day?

In all of this, we must keep in mind, even in the forefront of our search, the One who is the Lord of the Day. He claimed that title without any shame or hesitation (*Mark* 2:28). Wherever He is central in thought or worship or action, the process will be balanced and will bring glory to God. While the Day is the subject of this book, the Lord of the Day is the Master of the subject, and in His light shall we see light. Every topic must be traced to Him and find its destination in His glory. The study of the Day has its origin and its culmination in the 'dayspring from on high' who has visited us (*Luke* 1:78, KJV).

Now for the foundations which He has laid for our understanding. They, too, are signs of His goodness and grace.

2

Creation

2

Creation

THE SCRIPTURES CONSTANTLY connect the God who loves us and who has redeemed us with the God who created the heavens and the earth. To discover the foundations of the Day which God has appointed for Himself and for us, we must return to that beginning where God made all that is, for creation is foundational to belief and life.

There is a rhythm in the order of creation. The rhythm of God's creative work is enshrined in the Day set aside for His rest and ours. According to Genesis 2:1–3, He laboured for six days and then ceased from His labour. There, too, we are told by the Spirit of God that He not only rested on the seventh day, but that He blessed that Day and hallowed it. By blessing the Day we understand that God ordained that whoever uses the gift of the Day in accordance with His purpose and instructions will receive a blessing from Him. Listen as two eminent Hebrew scholars comment on the meaning of 'blessing': 'The divine act of blessing was a real communication of powers of salvation, grace and peace.'[1] It

---

[1] C. F. Keil and F. Delitzsch, *Commentary on the Old Testament*, vol. 1, p. 68.

has been objected that the statement in Genesis contains no command for observance on the part of man, on which point Patrick Fairbairn has written: 'The ground of obligation lay in the Divine act; the rule of duty was exhibited in the Divine example: for these were disclosed to men from the first, not to gratify an idle curiousity, but for the express purpose of leading them to know and do what is agreeable to the will of God.'[1]

God also sanctified the Day, that is to say, He set it apart from other days with a function that belonged uniquely to that Day. God performed a real act in this setting of the Day apart as holy. Listen again to the Hebrew scholars: 'Sanctifying was not merely declaring holy, but communicating the attribute of holiness, placing in a living relation to God the Holy One, raising it to a participation in the pure clear light of the holiness of God.'[2]

We learn from this to pattern the rhythm of our lives after God's. First rest, then labour, and then – rest. We also learn the divinely established proportion of work and rest: six to one. We are given the amount of time God set for our spiritual and physical rest – one day. He did not merely say, 'Take some time', but He gave us a whole day for the imitation of His cessation from labour.

The hallowing of the Day is not related to human sinfulness and the need of the Saviour, for the human race had not yet fallen into disobedience. The hallowing of the Day was an act of permanent significance, just as is the establishment of marriage. Although both the keeping of the Day and the institution of marriage were to suffer the ravages of sinful

---

[1] *Typology of Scripture*, vol. 1, p. 262.
[2] Keil and Delitzsch, *Commentary*, vol. 1, p. 68.

behaviour, they are not changed in character or in divine origin. They do not lose their true meaning with the increasing degradation of man. They are for this earth while men and women are allowed to live. They both become instruments in the hand of God as the plan for the redemption of the world unfolds.

We can picture the Day being observed in the Garden of Eden by a holy rest after the rhythm and pattern of the Maker. Though the work of Paradise was not arduous, the rhythm of work, followed by praise, meditation, and learning about God formed a delightful routine of life in the earliest picture we have of God's human family. Had we not sinned and brought the race into its fallen state, the Day would have yet continued as holy, and remained as a gift from God to His people for their well-being and for His praise.

So it is important for us now to remember that this Day was not inaugurated at some later time, but from the very beginning it was given. It is to be cherished by every creature made in the image of God as a concrete way of patterning life after the Perfect Life. It is to be regarded as a revealed sequence, and proportion, of labour and rest, and a means of growing in the knowledge and love of Him to whom we belong. We shall see that God, in inaugurating this Day at creation, is only commemorating His creative acts with this special gift for a time. What is crucial in creation is not so much the particular day as the rhythm, the proportion and the sequence. God will assign the Day according to His unfolding purpose in each era of His plan. Yet the essence of the Day is forever given and forever ours, that God at creation appointed a time of rest which is holy to Himself, forever.

3
Commandment

3

Commandment

IN THE COURSE of history between the creation and the
deliverance from the Egyptian bondage, the Sabbath
continued. Certain signs of it are found in the Book of
Genesis. The division of time into seven-day weeks is
evidence that the reckoning of days, revealed to our first
parents, remained in existence. And rest was ordered by the
Creator for the farmers' fields every seventh year to restore
the soil and to remind the Jewish people how fundamental
the Sabbath principle is in God's Word.

No doubt faith in God suffered from the impact of Egyptian
oppression and rigour. Perhaps the Day was almost lost to
the children of Israel. But God, through His servant Moses,
spoke to the people, restoring the Day after their deliverance
from Egypt (*Exod.* 16:23). The Creator was now the Deliverer,
and the Day was to be one of rest and rejoicing in remembrance of the miraculous redemption from the house of
bondage. It was sacred to the Lord. Even God's provision of
manna from heaven was in accord with the sanctity He had
placed on the seventh day, so that on the sixth day there was
a double portion, but none would appear on the seventh to

require the people's labour in its gathering. This is but one illustration of God's consistency, and reminds us again of the unity between creation and redemption. Exodus chapter 16 is in full harmony with Genesis chapter 2.

All of the mighty acts of God's deliverance led up to the giving of the Law at Mount Sinai. God never asks obedience unless He has first demonstrated His loving kindness and tender mercies. That is why He begins the pronouncement of the Law with the words, 'I am the LORD your God, who brought you out of the land of Egypt, out of the house of slavery' (Exod. 20:2). In God's self-revelation, the promulgation of the Law is a central act, because in it He discloses His nature to His creatures. 'You shall have no other gods before Me' (Exod. 20:3). By forbidding any other gods, He shows that He is jealous for the worship of His people, and by preventing any images in the worship of His name He discloses to us His own essential spirituality.

Likewise, His Law unfolds to us what is sanctified by God. His name, His worship, His spirituality, His Day, the family, property, human life, truth itself, and the singleness of the human heart are all set apart. The Commandments are hedges around the sacred things of God as well as pointers to what He is truly like.

The Commandments are a whole, a unit which cannot be divided (James 2:10). They build upon each other to give a complete picture of human duty and conduct balanced in its obligations both to God and man. Therefore the Fourth Commandment is not to be isolated from the others, but taken as a part of the whole, indicative of the nature and will of God, and pointing out what is sacred to Him. Stated in its totality, the longest of all the Commandments, it reads:

'Remember the Sabbath day, to keep it holy. Six days you shall labour and do all your work, but the seventh day is a Sabbath of the LORD your God; in it you shall not do any work, you or your son or daughter, your male or your female servant or your cattle or your sojourner who stays with you. For in six days the LORD made the heavens and the earth, the sea and all that is in them, and rested on the seventh day; therefore the LORD blessed the Sabbath day and made it holy' (*Exod.* 20: 8–11).

The Fourth Commandment does not designate the day to be observed as *the* Day. It restates what had already been exhibited at creation and what had probably fallen into neglect by a slave people. And behind the seventh day lies the Genesis principle of labour and rest and the proportion of time which is to be given to the special duties of the Day.

The Ten Commandments came from God through the Jewish culture and tradition, but they belong to the whole human family as the will of God for human life. It would be a gross mistake to think that, because the ceremonial aspects of the Day have been set aside with the coming of the Lord Jesus Christ, the Fourth Commandment itself, with its universal relevance, has been done away with. We do not treat any other Commandment that way. We find that the Book of Exodus prescribes severe treatment for one who steals and, though we do not apply that treatment today, the Eighth Commandment against stealing remains formative for our thinking and action. No one today sanctions stealing. Jesus reaffirms the Fourth Commandment when He expressly asserts that 'the Sabbath was made for man' – not for the Jew alone, but for man as man (*Mark* 2:27).

And the Decalogue is good for man. The holier one is, the happier he is. That is why the Ten Commandments are called the 'Moral Law'. Some laws God prescribes are good because He gives them. For example, the materials and rituals of worship outlined in the Ceremonial Law are good because God commanded them. But the Ten Commandments have an intrinsic goodness and benefit for us, and for that reason God commands them. It is this quality that constitutes the Decalogue the 'Moral Law'.

Of what purpose is the Law? No one of us is to think that by the keeping of the Commandments we can be saved. Our acceptance by God is only related to our cordial trust in Jesus the Christ as Saviour and Lord. Yet Christ Himself told us that He has not come to abolish the law but to fulfill it (*Matt.* 5:17). The law therefore has relevance in our lives because it forms the outline of God's will for daily living. It gives us a programme for action and for restraint. It tells us in ways that are objective and clear what God expects of us and what things will grieve Him. The Christian life, then, is the living out of the Commandments of God in positive and dynamic obedience to Christ under the power and guidance of the Holy Spirit.

Does the Fourth Commandment have meaning for the Christian today? Most surely, for in it God has revealed His will for the rhythm, sequence, and proportion of our lives. He reserves the right to attach the Day to the event which He wishes to exalt. In the commemoration of that event, the Day receives its meaning and is the vehicle of remembrance which He intended it to be.

The prophets of Israel viewed the Commandment as perpetual. They knew their old Jewish order would pass away, but they saw the new gospel order still preserving the gift of the Day. For example, the Prophet Isaiah wrote, under the leading of the Holy Spirit, a description of the new order that would be found in gospel times:

> Let not the foreigner who has joined himself to the LORD say,
> 'The LORD will surely separate me from His people.'
> Neither let the eunuch say, 'Behold I am a dry tree.'
> For thus says the LORD,
> 'To the eunuchs who keep My Sabbaths,
> And choose what pleases Me,
> And hold fast My covenant,
> To them I will give in My house and within My walls a memorial,
> And a name better than that of sons and daughters;
> I will give them an everlasting name which will not be cut off' (*Isa.* 56:3–5).

Here the Prophet sees the day, observed in gospel times, when the narrower restrictions of Jewish ceremonial law will be dropped. But the Day will be held sacred yet, for it is not part of the temporary Jewish order but of that permanent order outlined for us in the Commandments of God.

4
Christ

4
Christ

THE SABBATH EMERGED from the Mosaic period stronger and more lustrous than before. Enhanced by codification, it continued as the testimony of men and women to the existence and claims of God upon human life. The prophets fortified its sign by their vigorous insistence on its universal and perpetual obligation.

Yet when our Saviour appeared among us, the observance of the Day had been tarnished with the excesses of legalistic religion. Under the weight of man's burdensome teachings and the superstitious accretions of pharisaical religion, the Jews lost sight of God's purpose for His Day. The compassion of our Lord was aroused by this misapprehension and mistaken obligation. But to cite the compassion of Christ in support of non-observance of His Day is to misunderstand what He did in ministry among us.

There are eleven occasions noted in the Gospels in which our Lord's doctrine and spirit with regard to the Day are recorded. Rather than list them and explicate each one, I will attempt to summarize the features which characterize our Lord's understanding and use of the Sabbath Day.

It is clear that Jesus always honoured and kept the Sabbath. There is no occasion whatsoever in which He broke the Fourth Commandment. He performed miracles of healing on the Sabbath when the need and occasion arose. By this means He confirmed faith in His Messiahship. His activities on the Sabbath were never in violation of the Law, but always entirely in accordance with its meaning and purpose. Yet His actions on the Day were especially designed to deliver the Day from the barnacles which the Scribes and Pharisees had accorded it. It is also clear that at first there were no objections made to His activities on the Sabbath, but that they were made only later in His ministry as a covering for hatred of His divine mission.

These features help us to get closer to the real grasp of Jesus' own understanding of the Day. He honoured the Day as belonging to the Father, and proceeded to call Himself the Lord of the Day. Would He have claimed such a title if indeed He were about to abolish its significance and blessing to the world? Was it not in order to establish His authority and to relieve the Day of the excesses and misunderstandings which false and selfish religion had loaded upon it?

Did He not choose the Sabbath itself as the day of many of His miracles to show that the Day was made for man and not man for the Day? It was His purpose to show what kind of works are appropriate for Sabbath activity. Our Lord's words and actions on this Day expound the true meaning of the Fourth Commandment. They do not set that Commandment aside. Works of compassion and mercy are always works of which God approves.

Jesus Christ obeyed the spiritual intent of the Law, and lived out true Sabbath observance in His life. In His dying,

He carried with Him to the tomb the ancient Jewish Sabbath and on it He rested in the grave. This was God's abrogation of the particular day which had served until the new Moses was present and ready to lead God's people out of the deeper bondage into the higher liberty.

Then He rose from the dead to usher in a whole new order of creation. He is the second Adam and all who are in His loins spiritually are the new humanity, the sons of God by faith in Him. To this new race, the resurrection of Christ is crucial, for by dying and rising again our Saviour opens the way into the presence of God for believing and trusting sinners. Whoever has faith in Him shall live as He lives in His resurrection life.

Thus, the resurrection is the culminating event in the saving activity of our Lord Jesus Christ. It is something the Father does in Him and for us. Just as the first Moses had to be totally weakened in himself before he could be used by God to lead his people into freedom, so does the new 'Moses' (Christ) have to die before the Father can raise Him up and, by that resurrection, draw many to Himself. The resurrection is the cornerstone and the foundation of faith.

It was fitting that the Day should pass from the old Sabbath, which marked the Jewish deliverance, to the new Sabbath, marking the deliverance of the whole race from the bondage of sin and death. The first manifestation of the Sabbath was an invitation to the Jewish people to rejoice in God's creation and recognize His sovereignty over time. After the Exodus every Sabbath was also a call to Israel to remember that God is an Emancipator. Now each Lord's Day is a summons to believers to rejoice in the liberation that Jesus Christ has won for us by His death and resurrection, as well as to continue to rejoice in God's creative work.

Jesus laid the basis for the changing of the Day by calling Himself the Son of Man when He asserted His lordship over the Sabbath Day (*Mark* 2:27). 'Son of Man' is a title of deity, signifying that He, the Second Person of the Trinity, is the Person within the Godhead Who took human nature and human flesh. By asserting His deity He is claiming the right and the authority to transfer the observance of the Day to a new day with a new significance. 'The Lord of the Sabbath' means that He owns the Day and 'calls the hours His own'. He can use it however He pleases.

Yet how was this change to be made known? Jesus Christ always clothed an idea with His flesh first. He appeared to His disciples on Easter Sunday evening. He revealed Himself to them and they worshipped Him. Allowing a week to pass without revealing Himself again, He then appeared on the following Sunday to His disciples, including Thomas who had previously been absent and who had doubted.

At Pentecost, when He poured out His Spirit upon His church, He chose again the first day of the week, as if by this mighty action and gift to say to the church, 'This is the day which the LORD has made.' It was that very text from Psalm 118:24 which the disciples connected with the resurrection of our Lord, and the link between His resurrection and the new Christian Sabbath:

> The stone which the builders rejected
> Has become the chief corner stone.
> This is the LORD's doing;
> It is marvelous in our eyes.

This is the day which the Lord has made;
Let us rejoice and be glad in it' (*Psa.* 118:22–24; see also
Acts 4:11).

Our Lord Jesus explicated the Day most helpfully for us.
He expounded its injunctions as the True Legislator. With
His authority He voided everything that was contrary to its
genuine spirit and He left it for us as one of the great privi-
leges and distinctions of His Kingdom. By His resurrection
from the dead and the pouring out of His own Spirit on the
Day, He signified to us the change of day so that we could
commemorate His saving acts in our weekly day of rest. The
Day had memorialized creation and the deliverance from
Egypt, but something greater was now to be celebrated. The
New builds upon what is already revealed in the Old. All
that was required was the transference in the weekly cycle
from the seventh to the first day.

While the transference is indicated to us by the
resurrection appearances of our Lord, and in the pouring out
of the Holy Spirit at Pentecost, we can be sure that He made
the change of day still clearer to the apostles in His directions
to them. They knew Jesus was 'Lord of the Sabbath', its
Owner and Author, and it would have been impossible for
them to have made the change that they did in the apostolic
churches without His authority.

When the apostles began to assemble on the first day of
the week for worship and fellowship the practice had to be
at the direction of Christ. Paul's commitment to the new
Sabbath is demonstrated to us in Acts 20:6–7 where he
addressed the people of Troas on 'the first day of the week'.
Likewise he exhorts the Corinthians to set aside their gifts
on the 'the first day of every week' (*1 Cor.* 16:2). Again the

Apostle John speaks in Revelation 1:10 of being 'in the Spirit on the Lord's day'. In the picture of the primitive church assembling one day in seven – the Day on which Jesus had risen – we see how that Day remains specially set aside with blessings for mankind.

Yet the apostolic age was a transition time for many of the first believers who were Jews. They were accustomed to their Jewish festivals and only slowly dropped their observance. In this period some controversies arose because the question before them was, 'How far are we bound to the old Jewish festivals and holy days?' These too are described in the Scriptures as 'Sabbaths'.

It is in answer to this controversy that the Apostle Paul by the Spirit writes such passages as Romans 14:5–6, Galatians 4:10 and Colossians 2:16–17. Here the Apostle is addressing himself mainly to the festivals which were in dispute among them, and saying to them that those designated days in the Jewish calendar no longer have substantial meaning. They were of the nature of shadow, but the substance has come. The substance is Christ. But what he is speaking about as done away in Christ are the days in debate, not the Day agreed upon, the Lord's Day, the new Sabbath, when it is rightly observed. If the weekly Sabbath was observed only in an outward and ritualistic way, as it had come to be observed in much Jewish religion, it too would be included in this list of 'indifferent' kinds of holidays. Neither the Law nor the gospel would enforce that kind of practice. The real purpose of the Sabbath was to promote the holiness of God's people and foster communion with Him. Neither the weekly Sabbath, formally observed, nor the festivals of Jewish religion could do that.

In essence Paul said to them, 'These festivals no longer have any obligation for you. You have been set free from "days" in Christ, because their fulfilment has come.' But can that also apply to the weekly Sabbath, the Lord's Day? It would if the weekly Sabbath was *typical* in its meaning and therefore now fulfilled by Christ. But that is not the case. In its original establishment there was nothing typical, nothing that prefigured redemption, for sin had not yet entered and the need for a Saviour was not yet evident. When the Fourth Commandment was given, it still did not have a typical meaning. It was a restatement of the original institution of the Sabbath rest. Yet, as part of Jewish practice, it became a part of the types and shadows which paved the way for the Messiah. It was particularly the bodily rest of the Sabbath that became part of the symbolism of Jewish religion, as it looked toward its fulfilment in the Christ. But because of human sinfulness that aspect of the Fourth Commandment (bodily rest) was over-emphasized. It was necessary, then, in order to return to the true purpose of the Sabbath principle, holiness and spiritual communion, to place the old Jewish Sabbath among the list of things to be done away with, to inaugurate a new day of the week, and to give it a new name, 'the Lord's Day'.

There is a lesson here for us in this time. The same pitfalls of legalism and formalism which confronted our Jewish fathers in Old Testament times can steal away the richness and power of the Sabbath day. If we slip into thinking that a proper observance of the Lord's Day consists in refraining from work and giving only a modicum of time to worship and meditation on the Word of God, we shall have missed its real point in our lives. It is a day for communion with

God and fellowship with His people. These are dynamic and wonderful realities, but they require intentionality and planning. It is a positive kind of day, more than negative. It yields rich fruit when we put faith, sacrifice, effort and delight into it.

To do this the Holy Spirit must be our Guide and Helper. Without His help we shall have a barren observance of the principle of the Fourth Commandment. For this reason, while the Sabbath Commandment is binding upon all whom God has created, it can only be rightly obeyed by those who are trusting in the Lord Jesus Christ as their Saviour and have the ministry of the Holy Spirit to guide them in its observance. The words of John Newton remain true:

> How dull the Sabbath Day
> Without the Sabbath's Lord.

To suppose that the believer is set free from the Fourth Commandment and the Lord's Day would have been unthinkable to the early apostles. For example, one early church father, Irenaeus, wrote, 'On the Lord's Day every one of us Christians keeps the Sabbath, meditating on the works of God.' When the heathen would put the question to Christian martyrs, 'Do you keep Sunday?' the answer would be, 'I am a Christian; I cannot omit it.'

Thus Christ Himself is the great foundation stone of the Christian Sabbath. It is He who taught us its deepest meaning and showed by example the right use of its hours. It is He who ushered in its new significance by His own death and resurrection and it is He who enables us to keep it worthily to the Lord by the presence of His blessed Spirit in our hearts.

5

The Condition of
Humanity

5

The Condition of Humanity

THE LORD'S DAY has its signature on both the spiritual and the physical heart of humankind, for written deep within us is the divinely-given need for rhythm and rest. Days cannot be endless and weeks must give way to months. We long for variety, for relief from the steady pressures of business and learning. God has placed in our hearts the truth of His own ways, so that we might find it natural, in the best sense of that word, to obey His precepts on the Lord's Day.

It has long been recognized that the pulse of the physical body normally beats faster in the morning than in the evening, but after six days of this rhythm it beats slower in the morning. There the body is speaking to the spirit of men and women, that it needs the refreshment of a different day with new experiences and with rest for its weariness.

The physical heart of man requires the relief from steady pressure that there may be restoration of its powers. Heart disease is prevalent in these days. Many factors are responsible, but among these is the fact that the Day of Rest has not been given to human hearts. Sunday has become a day for activity rather than serenity, a day for recreation rather than for rest in God.

The mind of man needs the special stimulation which a day of reflection and prayer can bring. It works eagerly throughout the week seeking to solve business and family problems. On the Day God has given, it must be allowed to recharge itself by occupation with its own Maker. This special stimulation of the mind comes only from thinking God's thoughts after Him. A rubber band cannot be stretched always and still remain elastic. Neither can the human brain work ceaselessly unless there be periods of surcease in which it can be healed and released from the twisting problems of modern life. On this day, let the human mind be exercised in its highest function, which is praise and adoration, and meditation on God and the concerns which are His.

The appearance of a person reflects the beauty of the Lord who made him or her. But when shall lustre and light be better added to the countenance than on the Day appointed for refreshment? There is a Christlike countenance rarely seen these days, but which nevertheless exists and is available to those who will keep God's precepts for living. On the face are written the secrets of the heart, and if the very laws of God are being written within, then, according to His promise, the face will express the God of those laws (*Psa.* 34:5). The people of God need not concern themselves so much with feverish activity as with having faces aglow with the contentment and purity of the God they worship. Mirrored in the face will be that kind of healing quality afforded by properly observing the Day of days. We have already seen how the Day was given to our parents in Paradise and was necessary for their life before they fell into rebellion and death. If they, being innocent (and strong in their innocence) still needed a day of rest and worship for their well-being, how much more does fallen mankind, with its darkened mind and weakened body, require such a time for the restoration and refreshment of its spirit?

Both as creatures and as sinners we need the Sabbath. If the Day be lost, then the disease of sin within us gains more and more ground. Our restoration is arrested and our recovery endangered when this vital part of God's treatment plan is suspended. We are called more and more to die to sin and live to righteousness. The Day given by God is an instrument in His hand for that process of growth.

Some will argue that there is little time for spiritual growth, that the pressure of 'things', the tyranny of the immediate, keeps us from developing in knowledge or character as a godly man or woman ought. Yet to each is given a number of Sundays, perhaps as many as three or four thousand in a lifetime. On these holy days the needs of spirit and mind and body are to be met by attention to the Lord who gave them. But if Sabbaths are lost or frittered away, there may be no way to regain the benefits they would have given us.

The need is not only personal and individual. The social fabric also needs the mending of the Lord's Day. With the business places quiet, the offices silent, the populace has a new freedom to hear the words of instruction from the Law of the Lord. There is the chance to inculcate eternal truth and diffuse the true knowledge of the Lord to all classes of people. But when the Day is not held sacred, the very people for whom Christ came into the world will have the least opportunity to hear His Word and experience His love. It is the poor who will respond to rewards of 'double time' and extra work. It is they who must labour for the bread that perishes, and no lover of God should collaborate in robbing them of the ultimate Word which their souls need so deeply.

The Fourth Commandment has its echo in the nature of people and of things. What God has designed is integrated with what He has created. To experience His creation and neglect His Day is to miss one-half of His plan for us and to throw the segment we do experience into disorder and frustration.

When the Day God made is not observed, it is we who suffer by its neglect. A missionary to the Indians, in teaching the Sabbath principles to his flock, said, 'If you plant corn on the Lord's Day it will not grow. It will rot in the ground.' The Indians decided to put the preacher to the test. They planted a field of corn on the Lord's Day, watered and cultivated it carefully, and watched eagerly to see what would happen. Then they came and told the missionary that the Sunday field had a larger crop than any of the others. The missionary's response expressed a profound truth. 'Yes, God was kind and patient with you, but in the process your souls shrivelled within you.'

Embedded in time itself is the place of the Day. For why were weeks formed at all, but that one Day should be held sacred for the Lord?

Thus, dear reader, listen to God, listen to your own spirit, your body, your watch and calendar, look at the restless society in which you live, and vow to return to the Day from which you have wandered. It is like coming home, for it is natural to your need and will fit the unexpressed longings of heart and home.

6
Holiness

6

Holiness

HERE WE MOVE beyond the foundation around which we have been hovering to begin to build a sense of the structure of the Sabbath which God has designed for us. By structure I mean the outline, the shape – the thing for which the Sabbath was made and the features which give it form and substance. It is not, after all, an amorphous thing with no specifics to it. The Sabbath principle has a certain day assigned to it in each biblical instance and it has definite purposes and duties attached to it. It also has certain prohibitions, and they are specific and clear, yet adaptable in every age. That is the 'structure' of the Sabbath.

The commandment itself gives the outline of the design and substance. The purpose attached to why we are to remember the Sabbath Day is that we may keep it 'holy'. Holiness is the nature of its purpose and marks its character. Holiness here means that which makes God God. That which is cut off from all else, separated for the being and character of God. When we speak of God's holiness we mean His complete removal from all that is ungodly and His positive display of all divine and gracious attributes. He is utterly distinct from impurity or untruthfulness or uncertainty. He, alone, is God. Thus, the holiness of the Sabbath means that it is set apart to the God who is holy. It belongs to Him. He has put His name, His blessing upon it, and He maintains the right to order its use. To keep the Sabbath holy is to reserve its use for Him who is the 'Holy One'.

The Law of God must be understood both in its form and in its essence. While the form of Old Testament ceremonial and judicial laws has been abrogated, there is an underlying essence in each law which has an abiding relevance. In the Mosaic time, ceremonial washings prepared the people for the Sabbath and certain prohibitions built a hedge around the Day, preventing it from being encroached upon by mundane matters such as cooking and cleaning and travelling. These prohibitions were part of the ancient Mosaic ceremonial and judicial codes which were fulfilled and completed in the ministry and the sacrifice of our Lord Jesus Christ.

But the essence of these ancient laws remains. They fulfil a valuable function for us even now. They show us how the Holy God regards this Day, and they give us the outline of what He expects from us. Keeping His Day for Him in the ways He wants it kept is one of the most direct acknowledgements that a person can give of the existence and the holiness of God.

Keeping God's Day according to His direction changes a person or a people. If it is used in the pursuit of the heart of God and in doing His will, the Sabbath day leaves its mark. That is why the Sabbath is spoken of as a 'sign' of the Lord upon His people. So we read in Ezekiel 20:12, 'And I also gave them My sabbaths to be a sign between Me and them, that they might know that I am the LORD who sanctifies them.' The sign is directed to the heart of the person to reassure him of his part in God's covenant. But it also marks that person to others as one to whom the existence of God is a practical truth. The Sabbath is a sign that the people of God have received a covenant from Him, a sign the world can observe. It is therefore a sign of their holiness, not in the sense of their moral perfection, but in their being dis-tinguished from the rest of society and designated as belonging to God by covenant.

But God, in His economy, uses the same gift for more than one use. The Sabbath, meant to be a sign to the world of our consecration to God, becomes also the instrument of His making us into the people that we are to be – people in His own likeness. The holiness of God is not merely something to be reverenced from a distance, but a quality to be reproduced in the character of His people. But such a reproduction of His image requires much time and patience. For that reason the Lord's Day becomes a principal means of growing in Christlikeness for the people of God. It is an instrument of our sanctification. It is a way by which the holiness of God becomes gradually ours, because it affords us regular, protected opportunities for the cultivation of the ways and attitudes and works of Jesus Christ in our own lives.

What, then, is the nature of the Sabbath? It is a holy day, and to be kept holy. He owns the day. It is the Lord's – not ours. It must be treated as set apart to Him in order that we might grow like Him and be prepared for the service of His Name. When the Day is occupied with holy activities in a regular, conscious way, the Sabbath will become the sign to the world that it was intended to be.

Before dismissing the Sabbath, think clearly of this element of its nature: it is holy to the Lord. The Ark of the Covenant was holy, and Uzzah, the bearer of it, who tried to prevent its sliding to the ground, was killed instantly by the Lord. We are dealing with a central attribute of the eternal sovereign God who reveals Himself to us clearly. He has put His holiness on this Day and attached His own Name to it in the New Testament, designating it 'The Lord's Day'. To trifle with this Day, to pay it lip service, but not delight in its hours, is to be careless with the commands of the eternal God. That is why the command begins so solemnly, 'Remember the Sabbath Day, to keep it holy' (*Exod.* 20:8).

7
Rest

7

Rest

THE MEANING OF the word 'Sabbath' is crucial to our understanding of its structure. The root meaning of the word is 'cessation from labour'. In a sense, therefore, it means rest, but that is a secondary meaning. What is primary is the idea that the work is over and there is a period of pause which follows the labour.

This helps us understand God's Sabbath. He does not need rest, because He does not grow tired. Listen to the prophet Isaiah: 'The everlasting God, the LORD, the Creator of the ends of the earth does not become weary' (*Isa.* 40:28). He did not cease activity, but He did cease from His creative labours, and that is called His rest. This use of rest is reflected in the Epistle to the Hebrews, 'For the one who has entered His rest has himself also rested from his works, as God did from His' (*Heb.* 4:10).

It is important to realize that Sabbath-keeping does not mean inactivity. It speaks of the cessation which comes after labour. It is implied that what has ceased is that particular activity, and that other activities appropriate to the period of resting may be undertaken. Thus, Jesus spoke of the work that God is engaged in since His creative work was finished: 'My Father is working until now, and I myself am working'(*John* 5:17). Here Jesus cites His Father's sustaining activity on the Sabbath as ongoing, though in other places we note that God has ceased from His work.

There are, therefore, works that are appropriate to the Sabbath and works that are not. How shall one discern fitting activity for this sacred Day? Shall a list of rules be drawn up to govern them? No, the pattern for our conformity to the Law of God is in the Fourth Commandment. 'Six days you shall labour and do all your work; but the seventh day is a Sabbath to the LORD your God; in it you shall not do any work, you, or your son, or your daughter, your male or your female servant, or your cattle, or the sojourner who stays with you' (*Exod.* 20:9–10). God Himself, of course, is our example in keeping the Sabbath holy. See Genesis 2:2–3: 'And by the seventh day God completed his work which He had done; and he rested on the seventh day from all His work which he had done. Then God blessed the seventh day and sanctified it, because in it He rested from all His work which God had created and made.'

Exodus 31:17 interprets God's pattern for us: 'In six days the LORD made Heaven and earth, but on the seventh day He ceased from labour and was refreshed.' As Patrick Fairbairn has said, God *refreshing* Himself is a stronger expression: 'Figurative language this must, no doubt, be understood to be, yet it is not the less expressive of a great truth. The glorious Creator, surveying His own workmanship – looking with complacence on the product of His hands, and in the freshness of its joy and the prospect of its good order – finding satisfaction to Himself. How near does this show God to be to His creatures – in particular to the rational and upright portion of them! And must there not have been on *their* part the response of an intelligent appreciation and living fellowship? Must not man, endowed as he was with God's likeness, here also have communion with His Maker?"[1]

Man's first Sabbath was the first day of the week. It was the 'Eden Sabbath'. It began life and work with rest and refreshing in God, in the enjoyment of Him and His world. The Sabbath at the time of the Exodus from Egypt also ushered in a new period in the life of God's people. Life was to be a pilgrimage toward the land of promise, but was always to be begun with a day of rest and worship. The biblical pattern is rest – labour – rest, as a sequence, so that work fits between two God-given periods of rest and communion with God.

What is meant by the 'work' of God, after the ceasing of His work of creation? The work God was engaged in while He rested from His creative labour was at first the guidance and government of His people and His world. But since the Fall of man, God has engaged Himself also in the carrying out of His redemptive plan. He has finished His creative labour and ceased that activity on the day of His Sabbath rest. Still He works, drawing men and women to Himself, and caring for His church in the world. Following His example, the Christian man ceases from his labours in regard to the creation on the Lord's Day, and focuses on the works of worship, fellowship, and service.

[1] *Typology of Scripture*, vol. 1, p. 258.

The design of the Sabbath calls for a ceasing from our secular labours and our turning to the works that we shall be engaged in throughout eternity. Seven activities are described in Scripture as being part of our heavenly work: praising God, serving God, enjoying fellowship with Him and His people, learning of His ways and plan, meditating upon His precepts, administering His kingdom, and resting in His care. Are these work? In a certain sense they are, but they are the works to which we are called in this life as well as in the life to come. They are not the work proscribed in the Commandment. Instead, they parallel God's present activity after He is described as having finished His 'work'.

The shift to this kind of 'work' on the Sabbath Day forms a fitting preparation for life in heaven. Shall those activities be strange to us when we enter the presence of Christ or shall heaven be as a Sabbath continued without end, forever and ever? The right use of the Fourth Commandment is itself a way of making ready for life eternal with God.

The Commandments of God are laden with meaning for our lives. Implied in them is much more than lies on the surface. What does it mean not to engage in work that is similar to God's creative activity on the Sabbath day? It calls for refraining from conversation about our daily work, and from making plans for the week to come. It is more than simply not reporting for duty. It is to turn one's mind away from the things of this world, its cultivation and its care and its industry, so that the mind can be wholly occupied with the works of God.

Such an abandonment of the concerns of the week means that for a whole day one is not identified, labelled, by his work, but thought of only as a child of his heavenly Father.

Such a description is the more ultimate and lasting one, and God wants it repeated regularly in the ears of the person, so that he may know who he truly is and how God sees him in the midst of the labelling system of the world. That is not to say that he is known as a Christian only on the Lord's Day, but that on that day, in the context of worship and fellowship, his occupational labels are submerged under the recognition of him as a brother in Christ, a child of God.

Our example in interpreting this element of the structure of the Sabbath is Jesus Christ Himself. He refused to agree with His contemporaries who said that all work of any kind was unlawful on the Sabbath Day. At root, their trivial objections rose out of envy rather than concern for God and His Law. Yet Jesus showed that the works of healing and deliverance which He performed on the Sabbath Day were entirely within the intent of the Fourth Commandment. They were not out of order, but demonstrated clearly what God wanted to be done. They were works of 'necessity and mercy'; they did not require Him to take leave of holy activities on the Sabbath, but they were, first of all, signs of His deity, and always done for the well-being of others.

The Pharisees saw the Day as one of inactivity, perhaps even indolence. Jesus saw it as a resting from the ordinary activities of the six days, yet a day in which the works which God is now doing could be clearly engaged in with joy and great blessing. That is why He defended the works of the priests who minister in the temple on the Sabbath, as well as His own works of healing, feeding, and teaching.

The Sabbath is not enhanced by a Pharisaical interpretation of the meaning of the word. 'Sabbath rest' means the cessation of our regular labours so that the whole mind and heart and soul may be free for its more eternal, more significant, and more joyful work, the work of God. This, then, is the purpose of the Sabbath Day. The believer will ask, 'In what way can I leave behind the concerns of this world? How can I use the Sabbath hours to enter into the very labours which Christ would do now in the world?'

The rest which we gain from the Sabbath Day is not the rest of inactivity but the rest of change. As we engage in the activities of learning, praising, entering into fellowship, meditating, resting, administering, and serving, we experience in our hearts a refreshment greater than mere recreation could afford us. For the spirit in us is amplified by exercise, and the mind, wearied with pressures and competitions, is allowed to delight itself in its own Creator by thinking His own thoughts after Him.

The refreshment we experience is really a by-product, a reward that comes from obeying Him. When we truly copy His Sabbath activity, we shall delight in Him as he did in Himself. He revelled in the glory revealed in His marvellous creation. That is our chief Sabbath activity, revelling in the works of God in creation, providence and redemption – delighting in all that he has done. And doing so we are recharged and re-created more and more into His image.

Yet we remain in the world, and before us there will be the necessary meals to prepare and flat tyres to change as we are involved in these Sabbath activities. There will still be the man lying in the grass by the side of the road whom we must go back to help. Works of necessity and compassion are also a taste of Heaven. Such acts are not antithetical to our Sabbath observance but they are its fulfillment and point to the nature of the God whom we worship on this Day.

8
Others

8

Others

A LARGE PORTION of the wording of the Fourth Commandment is devoted to the concern for the Sabbath in the lives of those for whom one is responsible:

> 'In it you shall not do any work; you or your son, or your daughter, your male servant or your female servant or your cattle, or the sojourner who stays with you' (*Exod.* 20:10).

God works through established lines of authority, and thus, by commanding the preservation of the Day to those who are in charge of households and groups of people, He sought to ensure the possibilities of the Day for all His creatures. The principle embodied therein is most important. The human fabric is of one piece, and the observance of a regular day of holiness to the Lord and cessation from ordinary labour is an interdependent matter. Each person is not a law unto himself, but what each one does influences the lives of others.

God seeks by this section of His Commandment to guarantee that the whole community of faith will esteem His Day and thus make its blessings available to the least favoured and the lowliest of men and women, and even to the animals which they keep. God is no respecter of persons, and He intends that at least on this Day of the week, there may be a kind of equality which will foreshadow the equality that will be known in heaven.

Yet the wording may seem archaic to us, and irrelevant since few have servants or cattle. It is cast in ancient agrarian terms yet in its basic nature it communicates to people of every culture and situation. The point is clear: 'Don't take the Sabbath Day away from others, from anyone at all.' This refers not only to those who might be of the same faith and background as you are, but also to the stranger. Since the Commandments are to be taken positively as well as negatively, it might be stated this way: 'Do everything you can to protect and preserve the observance of the Sabbath for every life which you touch.'

Such a principle is only the application of the law of love to others because it guards their Sabbath Day. The human spirit is ever selfish and regards its own requirements before those of others. It looks out for its own comfort and well-being and disregards the needs and longings of others. That tendency must be checked in us, and the Fourth Commandment is God speaking to us and telling us that we are not to steal away the gift which He has given to all His creatures.

We must stop and think what we do to people when we force them to serve us on the Sabbath Day. We vote thereby for their being held in toil and ignorance. We raise up a barrier against the light of the gospel entering their souls. By our own example we are showing them that we are voting for the abolition of Christianity. In their presence we are denying the authority of God to command us in what we do and what we don't do. We erect an idol of a deity before them because we do not follow the true God in His orders to us. What we do is to give a lesson in practical atheism at that point in our lives.

Yet some will say, if I refrain from eating in a restaurant or causing a newspaper carrier to come to my home or purchasing fuel for my car, what difference will that make in a whole social structure geared to Sunday business? That question is irrelevant to the believer because what we are called to is obedience to the light which God has given us in His Word, not to estimating the results of that obedience. Were we to estimate that result we would discover that the observance or the disregard of a national Sabbath is made up of single acts repeated over and over again.

No nation has been permanently blessed and prospered that has disregarded the Fourth Commandment. In 1944 Prof. John Murray of Westminster Seminary preached a sermon, later judged one of the best preached that year, entitled 'God and the War'. His text was: 'When thy judgments are in the earth, the inhabitants of the world will learn righteousness' (*Isa.* 26:9b [KJV]). Murray said that, evil as the Hitler regime was, the war was also a judgment on the Allied powers, America included. He cited some of the sins for which America was being judged, among them the neglect of the Sabbath Day. Then the preacher made the amazing statement, 'One well-kept Sabbath would end this war.'

What can one person, one family, one church do? We can begin with the law of love and spare the Sabbath to other people so that they may have the freedom to enjoy this gift of God. If they do not make use of the Day as God intended, that is upon their own consciences, but if you or I take from them the precious privilege of meditating upon God and resting in His good providence on that Day, we shall give answer for that to Him who is the Lord of the Sabbath.

Parents need to see this section as outlining their duty to their own households. The heads of households are responsible for those under their roof. How that is to be carried out with children we shall come to in the closing chapters of this book.

9
Permanence

9

Permanence

THE COMMANDMENTS OUTLINE the nature of God. We have already seen how they reflect who He is and how we are to relate to Him and to each other. The Commandments are perpetually binding in that they describe God, and He does not change. We see this even in the Garden of Eden. There, false witness would not be tolerated (the Ninth Commandment), and the Day of the Lord must be kept sacred (the Fourth Commandment). Hence, God's authority becomes evident to us in the pages of the Bible before Sinai, witnessing to us that His sovereignty is exercised in His relation with man. Once given, the Commandments do not change, though ceremonial and ritual regulations may. The Moral Law is not only written in the Decalogue, but on the consciences of all men. Thus it is said, 'They show the work of the Law written in their hearts, their conscience bearing witness, and their thoughts alternately accusing or else defending them' (*Rom.* 2:15).

There is a certain timelessness about the Commandments. We are reminded that the Fourth Commandment is anchored to creation, not to the Exodus deliverance, though subsequent Sabbath teachings to the Jewish people do attach to the day of the miracle of release from bondage. But in the Fourth Commandment, which is a universal mandate for Sabbath observance, that connection is not made.

It must be granted that there are stretches of Bible history which contain no allusion to the Sabbath, but the same may be said for sacrifice which is not mentioned from the time of Abel until the Flood. We hear nothing of the important rite of circumcision for a period of eight hundred years, from the death of Moses to the time of Jeremiah. We have no mention of the Sabbath in the books of Joshua, Ruth, First and Second Samuel, and First Kings, yet this was during the period of the Mosaic Law, and we must assume that the keeping of the Sabbath was a part of Jewish life. Through all these centuries the seven-day week continued. It cannot be argued from the silence of certain parts of Scripture that God has changed His desire or modified His Law or withdrawn His precious gift.

The New Testament does not announce the change from the Jewish Sabbath (seventh day) to the First Day of the week in an explicit way, or attach to Sunday all the force of the Fourth Commandment. That fact has caused some to stumble and lose both the concept and the conviction that the Lord's Day is God's special Day to us in this era. What we find when we examine the New Testament is that the apostles began observing the first day of the week and calling it the Lord's Day. Anything related to the worship of God must have the authority of God to establish or change it. Without announcement the apostles began to treat the Lord's Day with the same kind of regard they would have given to the old Jewish Sabbath. Paul suspended his travels until after the Lord's Day (*Acts* 20:6–7). He also commanded the offering to be taken on the Lord's Day (*1 Cor.* 16:2). John was using the day for special meditation and prayer when the Spirit revealed the Apocalypse to him (*Rev.* 1:10). The apostles would not, could not, have made this fundamental change without the clear instruction of Christ. His appearing to them on that first Easter evening and then the following Sunday evening is the beginning of His instruction to the apostles. Certainly in the forty days between the resurrection and the ascension, in the hours of teaching which He gave them, He unfolded to them the new day of worship and taught them how to observe it.

The permanence of the Sabbath Day is a teaching of the Bible. God has given it to us in creation, in the Fourth Commandment, in the preaching of the prophets, in the example and teaching of our Lord Jesus Christ, and in the practice of the Apostolic Church, being led so directly and immediately by the Holy Spirit. He has never revoked His commands, but has kept them in force, as is underlined by the Lord Jesus Christ in the Sermon on the Mount (*Matt.* 5:17–20).

After the resurrection of Christ, and the abolition of the Mosaic ceremonial law in the death of Christ, the Fourth Commandment must find its fulfillment in a new Day. The memorial of creation, the commemoration of deliverance from bondage in Egypt as well, must be superseded as too narrow and provincial to serve the whole race. Even though the Exodus pilgrimage is used as a type of our redemption, it is superseded as the reason for the new Sabbath Day. Something far grander and greater has taken place – something that makes pilgrimage to heaven possible. The dying and rising again of our Saviour and His deliverance of us from sin and death are to be remembered on the Day of days. The transition is dramatized when the risen Lord Jesus meets with His disciples on that first Easter evening, shows them His hands and His side, and breathes on them the Holy Spirit, making of them a body of believers with the very life of God in them.

The writer to the Hebrews, speaking by the Holy Spirit, is a voice for the Sabbath when he undertakes to show how Christ is superior to the Old Covenant. In chapters three and four he deals with 'the rest' which God promises His people. That rest was foreshadowed in the Mosaic Covenant but not completely realized there. It has a greater depth to be known, and that is known in the rest given to weary hearts by the Saviour Himself. The rest He grants is greater than that which the figures of the Old Covenant could give. It is inner and eternal. So the writer says by the Spirit, 'There remains, therefore, a Sabbath rest for the people of God (Heb. 4:9).

The primary reference in this passage is to our final rest in heaven. But the week-by-week celebration of the Sabbath is a reminder and a preparation for heaven. The occupations of heaven are the same ones that God calls us to perform on His Day. Has the concept of a day been abolished for the believer in Christ? No, there remains a Sabbath rest for the people of God and the way to prepare for heaven is by the spiritual use of each Lord's Day.

Consider the permanence of the Day from the standpoint of the gospel era in which we live. Ought this time to be less favoured than the old time, by removing from us the great benediction and blessing of the Sabbath Day? Shall we be less blessed than David? Shall there be no day sacred to the Lord for His worship and praise and service?

Some would say that, since Christ has come, all days are sacred and no one day now is to be singled out as of unique worth and holiness. This view of the week has a certain appeal to it and there are many truly pious Christians who hold it. But we must also remember that in the case of Israel in slavery in Egypt, when all days were necessarily the same for them, the Sabbath Day was weakened, and perhaps lost to them for that time. If all days are the same, then no day is set apart as holy, and God may be robbed of the worship due Him. His people may no longer experience the rhythm He has built into the week and may lose the leisure to meditate on His nature and learn His ways.

The Sabbath Day is to be perpetually observed by the human race. It is God's great boon to the human family for all time, no less in this age than in the ages gone by. Yet it has fallen into neglect and misunderstanding. Its pattern must be rediscovered and cherished.

Its structure is that of holiness to the Lord, of ceasing from ordinary labour and thought, of preserving the Day for those around us, and of holding the Day to be permanently God's and permanently ours. Had the Saviour intended the abolition of the Day He would have said so to the Pharisees and to His followers. Instead He laboured to restore the Day to its original lustre and beauty. Ought not the silence of Scripture to be interpreted in the context of the whole revelation of God from Genesis forward? May we not apply to this matter the words of the Lord Jesus Christ when He said, 'If it were not so, I would have told you' (*John* 14:2)?

But the Scriptures taken together, in their broad sweep, point to this conclusion: God's Day remains for us. It has not been taken away, but enhanced by the work of the Spirit and the blessing of the Saviour.

10
Delight

10

Delight

THE BIBLE'S APPROACH to the Sabbath is positive, not negative. It calls for making the day a delight. No wife enjoys the time a husband sets aside for her reluctantly, as a duty. She is lifted when she sees him enjoying the time spent at her side. So does the Lord wish to see in His people a true anticipation and delight in the weekly return of the Sabbath Day. This is summed up beautifully in Isaiah 58:13–14:

> If because of the sabbath, you turn your foot
> From doing your own pleasure on my holy day,
> And call the sabbath a delight, the holy day of the LORD
>   honourable,
> And shall honour it, desisting from your own ways,
> From seeking your own pleasure,
> And speaking your own word,
> Then you will take delight in the LORD.
> And I will make you ride on the heights of the earth;
> And I will feed you with the heritage of Jacob your father,
> For the mouth of the LORD has spoken.

It is this delight which is the very core of the Sabbath. We have examined its foundation, the elements of its structure and now we must see, in practical ways, how we are to delight in this Day of days.

The chief delight of the Day is to be in God Himself. It is His Day. He created it and set it apart from the other days for Himself. He desires to be worshipped and magnified, for He is in truth the Centre of all things and the Reality from which all other reality springs. He is the only One who can say, 'I Am'. The heart of the Sabbath is the worship of the Lord God Almighty.

Jesus taught us that to do the works of God we are to believe on Him whom God has sent. Worship is the affirmation with others of the supreme worthiness and majesty of Christ. It is giving song to the emotions of the heart: 'Let the word of Christ richly dwell within you, with all wisdom teaching and admonishing one another with psalms and hymns and spiritual songs, singing with thankfulness in your hearts to God' (*Col.* 3:16).

It is important that on the Sabbath some of our worship be corporate. In this way we experience the added dimension of being carried along by the deeper devotion of godliness of others in the Christian community as drops of water are carried along by the waves of the sea. In the setting of public worship, God speaks to individuals as well as to the whole body. More is heard in the soul than is spoken from the pulpit or voiced in song. The presence of the whole congregation together is a way in which each believer may be 'present and accounted for' in the roll call of the kingdom of God.

This corporate expression of worship is an essential element in our Sabbath understanding. For if worship could be mainly or 'only' personal, then it would not be so necessary for one day – the same day for all – to be designated weekly for the public worship of God. But worship is not only personal; God has brought us into community for we are saved by the same blood, indwelt by the same Holy Spirit and share one faith and one destiny in heaven. There is a bond between believers that is strong and permanent. We are one in Christ, for we have all been adopted into His family and share Him as our elder brother. When we worship together we confess that we believe in the communion of saints, by which we mean that there is a mystical union that we enjoy. It is a union of love and caring, and we are ready to give our lives for each other. Since we have so great a unity, God ordains our gathering in worship and fellowship so that there may be a visible representation of His invisible kingdom here on earth. Such corporate worship becomes the foretaste of the kind of worship described in the book of Revelation where believers sing and praise the Lord in a great multitude 'which no one [can] count'.

A common description of the Lord's Day among the Puritans was 'the market-day of the soul'. They meant by this that whereas on other days spiritual food was available to them in limited amounts, on this Day there were great quantities and varieties of food for feasting. The tables were piled high with delicious things on this wondrous Day.

The whole day is given to us by the Lord for this, so that the time of worship shall not be wedged in between pressing engagements or worked into an already full schedule. There is to be, in God's design, the leisure to approach the place and hour of praise with a quiet and settled spirit and a pre-pared heart, a delight in the approaching of the first hour of the day, and a delight in reflecting on the day's experiences in its final hours. Following the benediction there must be an unhurried, calm and reflective atmosphere in which the truths of God can penetrate every part of the soul and mind and spirit. What comes before worship, and what follows it, are important to God and man. Wisely has the Lord made a buffer around the services, so that His people might make the periods of corporate worship the most important ones of the whole week. Like diamonds displayed alone, worship sparkles in beauty unrivalled by competing lights around it.

Christians who serve God in Muslim lands do not enjoy this spacious Sabbath. Though their national day of rest is Friday, most Christians in those lands still choose to worship God on Sunday, but then they must come to their churches on a brief leave from work or attend the service which meets after work is over for the day. In this, something is lost for them, yet they have counted it more important to worship together on the Lord's Day than to have the use of the whole of Friday for church services. One who observes their life together cannot help reflecting upon the privilege of Christians in lands where Sunday is normally available for worship.

We cannot use the Day in ways that do not contribute to the power of worship in our experience. We must give thanks for that providence which has given us the whole day for attendance upon the Lord's Word and His people, and not squander any part of it on activities that do not relate to the worship of God. There is a trend and tendency to give only a brief period of the day for worship and then to proceed with one's own pleasures. Some congregations even gather on Saturday evening so their members will have an uninter-rupted Sunday for other activities, though this is not the motivation in all cases. Where it is the motivation, one may feel that the weekly obligation is fulfilled and then fail to enjoy the spiritual quality and opportunities of the Sabbath Day itself.

The restoration of the biblical Sabbath would greatly reduce confusion in the churches over how worship should be conducted. Seeing the Sabbath's central theme as growth in holiness for the people of God will enable us to sift out elements that have crept into worship which do not cultivate holiness toward a holy God.

This emphasis on public worship does not, of course, mean that private worship is inappropriate on the Sabbath. Private spiritual duties form the prelude and supply the energy of public worship. When each believer comes to the house of the Lord with his own cup already filled with the good things of God found in quiet prayer and meditation, then the gathering is itself an outpouring of the mighty river of God's Spirit. Private reflection and communion with God should begin the Lord's Day and close it, and be the intermittent activity through the hours of the Sabbath.

For, like the tree which has its roots deep in hidden places and yet stretches its visible foliage out into the sunlight, so does the Christian need personal and quiet communion with God as well as corporate joining in the worship of God with other believers. The Sabbath is God's making room for both of these and interweaving them in a strong and lovely pattern of personal Christian living. Right use of the Sabbath aids the development of the devotional and the worshipful life in the hearts of the people of God.

The key is the word 'delight'. That means reflecting the mood of the Psalmist: 'I was glad when they said to me, "Let us go to the house of the LORD"' (*Psa.* 122:1). Having anticipation in the soul for the Sabbath to come is to join the ranks of those like David who panted after God, longing to come and appear before Him. It is to be in concert with Moses with whom God spoke face to face. It is to resemble our Lord Jesus Christ who retired from the crowds in anticipation of fellowship with His heavenly Father. True worship is the central focus of the Sabbath, and to surround it with private communion with God is to 'call the Sabbath a delight', as God has called us to do.

11
Service

11

Service

IT FOLLOWS FOR US TO EXPLORE the implications of 'delighting' in the Sabbath; that is, the right use of the Day set apart by God for Himself. To remain merely idle is not delighting in the Day. We have already discussed the true meaning of 'Sabbath rest'. It is a day of resting from our ordinary labours, but not of ceasing from the works of God which benefit His creatures.

What then are the right kinds of activity for this day? The key is found in Jesus' use of the Sabbath. He deliberately chose it for the accomplishment of certain healing miracles. Obviously He felt it appropriate to free from illness on the Sabbath Day one who had been bound for many years by Satan. Likewise He said that 'the Sabbath was made for man, not man for the Sabbath' (Mark 2:27). Here He taught us that the Sabbath was not an end in itself, but a means of obeying God. Jesus appears to be active, not indolent, on the Sabbath, indicating to us the kind of use to make of God's special day.

What does our Lord's example mean in our time? It suggests that the Lord's Day be full of the right kind of works done in the right spirit. Humanitarian works alone, done without God's Name and honour at the centre, would not keep the Day holy, and would not bring glory and honour to Him. But works 'for man' which are done in Christ's Name, and which are motivated by His Spirit, may be following in His footsteps.

What does it mean to say, 'The Sabbath was made for man'? Is it not God's saying to us that He wills the Day for the upbuilding of mankind and the mutual ministry of one to another in the human family? Not that the Day should become man-centred, but instead that its primary direction be kept towards the Lord. This becomes for us a guideline in our use of our time on the Lord's Day. Who are the people whose lives we have been wanting to touch? Which neighbours has God placed heavily upon our hearts? Where are the forgotten members of our churches? Do the patients in the nearby veterans' hospital receive visitors? Recently Charles Colson visited a western city where a large federal prison is located. Speaking to a group of citizens during his stay there, he found that none of them had even been inside that prison! Perhaps the churches had not empowered and motivated their people on the Lord's Day to reach out to those in prison.

Here the church must assist without being itself a part of the problem by crowding her schedule so full that there is little time for rest, reflection or service. Opportunities for worship and instruction and Christian fellowship must be provided by her officers. The morning hours ought to focus the attention of the believing community on the Lord of the Sabbath and the resurrection of the Lord. As the sun sets and the Day is giving way to the week's work before it, let the church find its way again to the house of the Lord for rejoicing in the risen Christ who will go with them through whatever is ahead. The Christian needs to be empowered, uplifted, refreshed and filled with the Spirit from the worship, fellowship and service of the Lord's Day.

It is a Day of rejoicing. It commemorates the resurrection of Christ. It is festive, full of singing and praising and glorifying the God who has brought life out of death through the gospel of Christ. Nothing should be done to make it burdensome or sad, but, with creative and imaginative spirits, let the church find happy paths of worship, fellowship, and sacrifice which will lead her people into the experience of a truly Christlike Sabbath.

12
Instruction

12

Instruction

THE VERY FOUNDING of the Sabbath Day was instructive to the human family. Its regular occurrence was a perpetual reminder to the earliest of God's creatures of His existence and His design for human life. Thus in the nature of the Sabbath itself, instruction is present. The Christian today needs to husband the precious hours of the Lord's Day for personal growth in knowledge. Never before in the history of the Christian Church has there been such a plethora of helpful books and magazines to assist us in our spiritual journey. Yet the pressures of society and the rigours of earning a living prevent blocks of time from being allocated to the grasp of the great truths of God from Scripture and the writings of other Christians. Sunday is the day for reflection and growth through becoming acquainted with the Church Fathers, the Reformers, the Puritans, and significant contemporary authors.

Every believer has areas in his own life where ignorance prevails over illumination. But God has provided regular periods of quiet in the division of time in which these pockets of ignorance can be flooded with the truth-bearing light of Christian knowledge. Does one desire a deeper communion with God? Let him turn to such a book as J. I. Packer's *Knowing*

God. Does one misunderstand the basis and implementation of Christian liberty? Spend some time with Calvin's *Institutes of the Christian Religion*. Does another believer have difficulty seeing the unity of the Old and the New Testaments? Vos' *Biblical Theology* would be a study for a year, refreshing the mind and spirit with deep insight into the Old Testament's preparation for the New. If one is experiencing difficulty in the practical application of his Christian faith to work, or marriage, or church life, then there are modern books that give practical ways for applying God's truth in specific situations. An older classic is B. M. Palmer's *The Family*. Thus, Sunday becomes a day for Christian learning.

In the home the husband and father has been established as 'prophet'. We know this because he is instructed to be as Christ to his wife. Christ functioned as a prophet, a priest, and a king, giving thereby a pattern by which the husband can understand his roles toward his family. In private, he intercedes for his family in prayer. In the long-range decisions and crucial choices as a family, he functions as king. But wherein is his prophetic role? This has been largely lost and the lack of time is often cited as the chief reason. But God has given us a day for the teaching and instruction of our children. On this day, we are to gather around us those whom God has given and pass on from one generation to another the truths of revelation.

The husband who has himself learned how to use the Day will be in a position both in understanding and example to lead his family in the right use of these sacred hours. He will have gathered some understanding of the Bible and of Christian truth from the books which he has read. In many countries, a visit to a Christian bookshop can supply him with the materials he needs to teach the Childrens' Catechism or the Shorter Catechism, as well as Bible study books and great

Christian biographies. The world of nature is full of illustrations helpful in human life. The ways of the animals put before us by God as examples of certain character qualities which we are to avoid or to emulate. Much of this rich learning is untapped as a helpful resource by the modern father because the Lord's Day is pre-empted by sports or secular activities.

In the single-parent home, if the pressure of duties prevents a mother or father from having this ministry on the Lord's Day, perhaps they might join with another family and take part in these activities on a Sunday afternoon.

Let the evening *before* the Lord's Day be as restful as possible in order that maximum strength be available to the family for the instructional use of the Day which God has made. If but one hour per week was devoted to this kind of home instruction, lasting memories and eternal benefits would accrue to the children. Then would be fulfilled what is written in 2 Timothy 3:14–15 : 'You, however, continue in the things you have learned and become convinced of, knowing from whom you have learned them, and that from childhood you have known the sacred writings which are able to give you the wisdom that leads to salvation through faith which is in Christ Jesus.'

Here father and mother can collaborate in the instruction of their children. In the private planning times they have together, the use of the Lord's Day ought to figure as a main topic for discussion. Let them set topics together and divide responsibilities so that both of them are involved in the work which crowns all their other labours. Often a mother can make an interesting passage from the Bible or other book live in the minds of the children. A father may have a gift for explaining, or inventing creative ways to communicate a truth in other ways. Let each exercise his or her own gifts in a way that unites the family and opens up the world of Christian truth for young minds to enter.

The church can help by restraining herself from over-scheduling on the Lord's Day, allowing room for families to have time together. Likewise she can have in her foyer a display of Christian books and materials for fathers or mothers to teach children. Some will object that books ought not to be sold on Sunday. But that objection will not hold when tested in the light of Scripture. The passage often cited, where Jesus drove the moneychangers from the temple (*Matt.* 21:12) is not pertinent. There the temple authorities were capitalizing on the plight of pilgrims who were far from home with no offerings that would meet the requirements of the temple. They bought and sold at profit to themselves and victimized the worshippers of the Lord. It is this which is wrong and which would be wrong on any day on which it was done. Jesus makes no allusion to the Sabbath. But to make available for purchase the materials that a parent could use with his or her children on the hours of Sunday is a helpful and holy ministry and every church ought to engage in it.

Mention has not been made here of the ways in which the church herself can assist learning on the Lord's Day, because that is adequately covered in volumes on Christian Education. Only let the church remember that she is the supplement to the family's programme of instruction. Let her seek to supplement what families are doing rather than to be a substitute or rival to it.

When the Lord's Day is used for learning the things of God then there is great blessing in the home and the church. Then the human mind is being used as God intended, and there is the fulfillment of the commandment, 'Remember the Sabbath Day to keep it holy.'

13
Antinomianism

13

Antinomianism

THE SABBATH HAS been shown to be perpetual in its obligation upon us. The Fourth Commandment, like the others, was placed in the Ark of the Covenant, while the ceremonial Sabbath rules of Jewish life were not. The Commandments are cited in the New Testament as still binding upon the believer (see Ephesians 6:2, Revelation 12:17). The Commandments were given with great display of thunder and lightning and were written in stone by the very finger of God to underline their enduring nature. The ceremonial and judicial laws were inscribed only on parchment, to show their temporary nature. Among the great Ten Words for life stands the Sabbath Commandment and its force is undiminished in this age.

The particular day, we have said, is not of the essence of the Commandment. The transition was made from the day marking the Exodus deliverance to that which marks the redemption completed in the resurrection of our Lord Jesus Christ. The apostles, the early church and the church fathers all agree in their observance of the first day of the week as the Sabbath.

The Christian Sabbath has been acknowledged in every period of the church's history. Yet its preservation has always been a struggle, for a latent atheism and rebellion in the heart of man keeps asserting itself against the divine mandate of our Sabbath-keeping. The enemy of the gospel also unleashes all his strategy and strength against the Day which God has appointed because he knows that, when the Sabbath Day is obliterated in the human heart and in society, the work of Christ is greatly impaired. Thus, he concentrates His energy on the task of making this Day just like every other day. But where is God, who instituted this grand and glorious surcease in the schedule of His people? He permits His truth to be assailed in different ways in order to try and prove the faithfulness of His people. Thus, in this hour when the Day is about to disappear from view, God is at work speaking to different segments of His people, recalling them to its due observance and its holy use. Here and there, in places and by voices apparently unconnected with each other, there is a renewal of interest in and prayer for the observance of the Day.

God likens the profaning of the Sabbath Day to idolatry. The modern Christian would shun idolatry with all his being, yet he allows the Sabbath to go unsanctified in his life and home. Ezekiel wrote, under the power of the Holy Spirit, 'They rejected my ordinances, and as for My statutes, they did not walk in them; they even profaned My sabbaths, for their heart continually went after their idols'(*Ezek.* 20:16). The same sequence is true today. While we do not recognize them as idols, many pleasures and possessions fill that place in our lives. If the Sabbath is restored there will be a refusal to bow down to them and we shall be awake to the danger of these idols. By having to separate out in our lives what is appropriate for Sabbath activity, we will recognize what a stronghold the pleasures and ways of the world have taken upon our minds and imaginations. Thus, Sabbath-keeping is God's revealer of idolatrous practices among His people.

One of the great dangers for Christians in this hour is the new antinomianism. This ancient heresy, condemned long ago, has raised its head again and has seduced us to follow its ways. It calls for the abandonment of Law in the Christian life and the uplifting of 'grace'. But what this generally means is that Christians are guided by circumstance and desire rather than by principle and conviction. Scripture ceases to rule. This has brought about moral disaster in many a home and church and soiled the pure name of Christ. The element of truth in antinomianism is enlarged out of its scriptural balance. There is no question that salvation is through faith in the Lord Jesus Christ, apart from obedience to the Law. The Letters to the Romans and the Galatians are written with this specific objective, that no one should think that the keeping of the Law is necessary for salvation or contributes in any way to it. God may use the Law as a 'mentor' in keeping us from gross sin, even preserving our lives until we are at the place where we embrace Jesus Christ alone as our only hope of salvation (*Gal.* 3:24). Still the purpose of Christ's coming, His death and resurrection was to redeem those who were under the Law (*Gal.* 4:5). If the Law, in any of its forms, could save the sinner, Christ's coming and His death would have been unnecessary and a tragic waste.

Yet the Law is good and holy (*Rom.* 7:12). It is a description of God's nature and an outline of how He wants life to be lived in His world. The gospel leads to the fulfillment of Law.

The gospel is not lawless. As Paul writes in Romans 3:31, 'Do we then nullify the Law through faith? May it never be! On the contrary, we establish the Law.' The result of the new life that Christ gives to the repentant and believing sinner is the disposition of friendship with God, with the desire to obey His Law. There is the confidence that this is the shape of the life God wants for His children, as well as the sense that one pleases God and shows love for the Lord Jesus by obeying His commandments. Such a desire to please God does not mean that the person has come 'under the Law'.

Thus, the Christian person is under obligation to the moral Law. His repentance involves obeying God where before He had disobeyed Him. Obeying God's Law is obeying God. That is why the gospel does not make void the Law, but rather fulfils it. How foolish it is to think of the Law as irrelevant to the believer, when the whole purpose of the gospel he loves is to put him in a frame of heart that is able to live life as God has outlined it in His holy Commandments.

Not all Christians who de-emphasize the Sabbath do so because they are antinomian in their thinking and behaviour. But in some cases the Sabbath Day has been eroded because of the revival of this ancient heresy. The modern Christian may wonder about the validity of the Sabbath Commandment to him, since he has been redeemed by Christ, apart from the Law. What does an ancient Law of God have to do with his living out the new life Christ has given him? But without realizing it, the one who thinks in this way may be invaded by the spirit of lawlessness. He is in danger of forgetting the words of our Lord Jesus, 'He who has My commandments and keeps them, he it is who loves Me; and he who loves Me shall be loved by My Father, and I will love him and will disclose Myself to him' (*John* 14:21). To Jesus Christ, devotion to His Person was not simply a matter of an inner feeling, or mental attitude, but rather a concrete matter of doing the things which He commanded. At this point the antinomian loses touch with Christ as He really is and follows an idol of his own making.

To return to the true Christ means a return to obedience to the Law of God. It was this which Nehemiah sought to bring about in ancient Jerusalem. He found the people buying and selling and moving merchandise on the Day of God. With determination and great courage he confronted them and insisted on obedience to the great Law of God, and the Scripture holds him in great esteem for his work. Such simple obedience to the Law of God is required today if we are to recover the loyalty to Jesus Christ which He demands of us.

14

Consummation

14
Consummation

THE CRY OF the age is, 'Everybody is doing it.' Too many
Christians fear that to keep the Sabbath today would be to
isolate themselves from the mainstream of life, so they draw
back in self-consciousness and fear. Unbelievers do not keep
the Sabbath partly because they do not see its observance on
the part of their Christian neighbours. They see that
Christians make no special attempt to set aside the Day with
reverence for rest and worship. They hear their Christian
associates discuss the Sunday football game just as non-
believers do. They notice their Christian neighbours bringing
in the Sunday paper the first thing on Sunday morning. The
distinction between church and world has been erased. The
Sabbath was meant to be a sign between the world and the
Christian. Remove the sign and the distinction is removed
as well.

The call is to a radical obedience that begins with a radical
repentance. It was for this that Nehemiah called. We have
broken the holy Law of God. We have despised the sacred
and lovely gift He has given to us. We have thought more of
the approval of our children and our neighbours, and of our

own comfort, than we have of the Commandment of the
eternal God. We are undone and we dwell among a people
who are undone. Judgment must begin at the house of God.
Revival may begin when God's people confess their misuse
of the Day of God and turn again to it, not in pride and
hypocrisy but in humble and quiet use of the Day in the ways
shown forth in the Word of God.

Someone will say, 'Why bother with the Fourth Commandment when greater, more grievous sins abound? Why start
there?' It is true that no commandment of God is to be
stressed to the exclusion of others, but the Fourth Commandment is part of 'the first of all the commandments' (Mark
12:29). It concerns the love of God. Its true observation will
set in motion an examination of our entire life. It is like a
lens for the scrutinizing of hearts and attitudes. It prompts
the removal of the idols that have taken up residence within
us. Thus we may begin here. To pass over this Commandment removes a means for the restoration of all the rest of
our lives.

The starting place is the heart of a believer. Secretly, God
brings home to you by His Spirit that which is shown openly
in the Scripture – the command of the Sabbath. It is one of
the principal functions of the Spirit to write this Law upon
our hearts. As He does this, purpose in your heart to delight
in the Lord's Day and to preserve it from all encroachments
of the world. It is not without reason that the Fourth
Commandment begins with the words, 'Remember the
Sabbath day, to keep it holy.' The temptation is to lose it, to
forget it. The word 'Remember' calls for an eternal vigilance
and a strong effort to hold fast to the Day which God has
called His own.

The starting place is in the spirit of a person, and we must go from strength to strength in the understanding and holy employments of the day. Then we must teach our young people so that a generation of godly offspring will be able to follow us. Here we are called not only to instruct about the Sabbath but also to govern our own children, so that their lives are managed with reference to the Commandments of God. We would not allow them to murder or steal, yet we may encourage them to deliver papers or give themselves to studies on Sunday.

'How can a young man keep his way pure? By keeping it according to your word' (*Psa.* 119:9). The Lord's Day is the special time for a young person to grasp the things of God and to meditate on the will of God for His life. Parents, teachers, and pastors, by example and by guidance and governing, need to be the agents of the Holy Spirit in fashioning the new generation in the ways of the Sabbath of the Lord. Yet all this ought to be done in the spirit of a delight and a privilege. The Day is a blessing, not a burden or a restriction. 'His commandments are not burdensome' (*1 John* 5:3).

Let those who follow us see what a gift God has given, how He has freed us from our usual toils and diversions this one day, that we may enter into closer communion with Him. As our youth plan their life work or accept part-time jobs, they need to be counselled about the Sabbath Day, and reminded that many who have gone before them have turned down work and pleasure on the ground of the Fourth Commandment.

But the Sabbath has a future dimension that we must not miss. The Sabbath on earth is a foretaste and a preparation for the eternal rest, the eternal Sabbath in heaven. And that Sabbath to come will make this present one pale in comparison – *this* is but the down payment, *that* the treasured final possession. *This* is but the first fruits and *that* the full harvest.

But can we in the thick of the business of living give much time or attention to the Sabbath reserved for us in the world to come? Are we able to handle more than one world at a time? An answer to this is in John's description of his own Sabbath observance. He was 'in the Spirit on the Lord's Day' (*Rev.* 1:10) It was then that the vision of future things was given to him. Can we also seek to be in the Spirit and to contemplate heaven each Lord's Day, reminding ourselves of what the occupations there will be, delighting in the prospect of the Saviour's face, and His voice like the sound of many waters? It was Richard Baxter who told us to let heaven have more share in our Sabbaths, where we must shortly keep our everlasting Sabbaths.

We are always in danger of forgetting that the weekly Sabbath is but an emblem standing for a far greater reality. We could so easily be fixed on the emblem that we miss the tremendous joy that it represents for us. One day the emblem will be replaced by the reality, and then we shall see the truest meaning and glory of the weekly Sabbaths which have been only preparation for the eternal rest to which Christ bids us.

And how joyous it will be to enter into the eternal Sabbath activities in their full power and glory! Our praising will take on a vigour we have never known before. Our serving God will be without an admixture of other motives and we will marvel at the effectiveness and joy of it. Our fellowship with

God and His people will show us to have become true lovers and we will rejoice in that. Our learning experiences will take us to the heart of a subject and to a depth of understanding that will be utterly amazing to us and we will give thanks. Our meditation on His precepts will produce insights that will make us stand in awe of the wonder of His truth. Our administering of His kingdom will help us to understand what has been the meaning of our present life all along. The deep rest we shall know in the heavenly Sabbath rest will make our weekly rest shallow by comparison. But there is a continuity, as well as a contrast and a comparison, between the Lord's Day and the heavenly rest. It is the same God who has given us the Day here who will give us the eternal Day of glory.

When shall we begin this reformation of the schedule and rhythm of life? God calls us to it now. The hour is already very late and the time is short. Only a few Sabbaths are left for some. How will they be used?

Yield, my Christian friends, to the truth of the Word of God! Accept the gracious influences of the Holy Spirit upon your heart now! Repent of the way you have wasted the Day, and purpose in your heart before God to give Him the Sabbaths that remain! Decide in your heart how firm and strong will be your Sabbath discipline. Ask God to re-establish the Day in your heart, your home and your church!